U.S. Department of the Interior
Office of Inspector General

AUDIT REPORT

U.S. Department of the Interior

Radio Communications Program

Report No. C-IN-MOA-0007-2005

January 2007

EXECUTIVE SUMMARY

WHAT WE FOUND

The U.S. Department of the Interior (DOI) has an unsafe and unreliable radio communications environment that jeopardizes the health and safety of DOI employees and the public.

The results of this audit demonstrate that radio communications in DOI are unsafe and unreliable because:

> The poorly maintained infrastructure poses physical safety hazards, and does not support reliable communications.

> The new radio technology adopted by DOI does not effectively meet users' needs.

> DOI has a fragmented radio communications program that fails to connect the two critical components – infrastructure and equipment.

Technical studies have identified over 100 DOI radio sites in poor or hazardous condition. These conditions result in physical safety hazards that pose an immediate risk of injury or death to employees and the public. Safety hazards include insufficient grounding of towers, improperly installed equipment, overloaded radio towers, and lack of security fences. The poorly maintained infrastructure also contributed to unreliable radio communications, putting employees at risk during emergency situations. This situation has primarily occurred because of decentralized management of the radio communications program.

We found that the mandate issued by the Office of the Chief Information Officer (OCIO) in 1998 to purchase advanced digital radios failed to consider user needs, did not include adequate training, and contributed to DOI's failure to meet the federal requirement to transition to narrowband technology by January 1, 2005. Our audit identified approximately $25

DOI HAS OVER 100 RADIO SITES IN EXTREMELY POOR OR HAZARDOUS CONDITION, WHICH POSE AN IMMEDIATE RISK OF INJURY OR DEATH TO EMPLOYEES AND THE PUBLIC.

WHY WE DID THIS AUDIT

Effective radio communication is critical to employee and public safety and the efficient management of our public lands.

The Inspector General has identified radio communication as a critical component of Health, Safety and Emergency Management, which was one of DOI's Top Management Challenges for FY2004 through FY2006.

Our audit objective was to determine whether DOI and its bureaus effectively managed the radio communications program.

i

million in unnecessary expenditures because of this mandate. Additionally, we estimate that one bureau could still save approximately $10.5 million if it were exempted from this mandate.

Two separate DOI entities hold responsibility for radio equipment and radio communications infrastructure. Equipment needs are subject to one internal DOI process, while infrastructure needs are governed by another. As a result, both components necessary for the DOI radio communications program are ineffective.

Without fundamental changes to the radio communications program, DOI will continue to jeopardize the safety of its employees and the public and squander resources. Given the critical nature of radio communications and the seriousness of the issues we identified, we believe that the radio communications program remains a material weakness for DOI. In 2004, however, DOI downgraded the radio communications program from a Departmental level material weakness to a bureau level material weakness for only two bureaus, without conducting the required Management Review.

To address deficiencies in its radio communications program, DOI should consolidate management and funding of both the radio equipment and related infrastructure under the OCIO. The OCIO should then appoint a credentialed project manager to oversee the program and develop a Department-wide plan for radio communications. Our report provides a series of recommendations intended to help improve the safety and reliability of the program, better manage costs, and meet the narrowband requirement. Additionally, as part of our audit, we identified suggestions from DOI employees in the radio communications program and best practices used by other federal agencies to improve program operations. The OCIO should consider these suggestions and best practices in developing its comprehensive management plan.

DOI's response to the draft report, included as Appendix 6, agreed that improvements can be made in the areas highlighted in the report; however DOI expressed concern that our report did not reflect recent progress made and the current status of the radio communications program. DOI provided specific examples where progress was made by the Bureau of Land Management (BLM) and the Fish and Wildlife Service (FWS). We updated our testing to address these examples and found that DOI's assertions of improvement were not accurate. DOI disagreed with all but one of our recommendations. Based on DOI's response and to clarify our intent, we revised two recommendations. The remaining recommendations are unchanged from our draft report.

TABLE OF CONTENTS

Cover Photo Credits
Forest photos provided by the National Park Service
Tower photo provided by [Exemption 6]

INTRODUCTION

This report presents the results of our audit of the Department of the Interior's (DOI) radio communications program. The objective of our audit was to determine whether DOI and its bureaus are effectively managing the radio communications program. Specifically:

➤ Are they updating aging and unsafe radio infrastructure?

➤ Are they using their resources efficiently?

➤ Has the mandate to transition to narrowband technology been met?

BACKGROUND

DOI and its bureaus use land mobile radio (LMR) communication systems to carry out critical day-to-day operations. Some of DOI's activities that use radios include law enforcement, fire fighting, seismic monitoring, park management, and water management.

GENERAL RADIO COMMUNICATION SYSTEM OPERATIONS

An LMR system is comprised of equipment, such as handheld radios, vehicle-mounted mobile radios, dispatch consoles, and one or more radio repeaters. A repeater is a device that receives a signal and then retransmits it to allow the signal to travel greater distances. Depending on the size of the geographical area covered, an LMR system can have one repeater or a network of repeaters. The dispatch console is typically located at an organization's headquarters and is used to communicate to all the system users through a network of repeaters. **Figure 1** illustrates a traditional LMR system.

WHEN A USER TRANSMITS A MESSAGE ON HIS/HER RADIO, THE REPEATER RECEIVES THE TRANSMISSION AND THEN REBROADCASTS THE COMMUNICATION TO OTHER HANDHELD AND MOBILE RADIOS WITHIN THE RADIO SYSTEM.

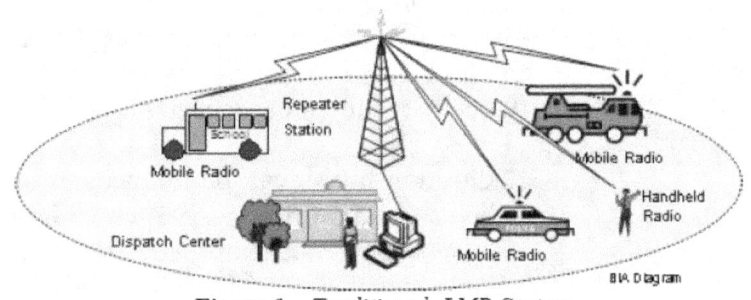

Figure 1 – Traditional LMR System

1

LMR systems also require towers to hold the repeaters and protective housing to shelter the radio equipment. The towers and housing required to operate the radio equipment are referred to as the radio "infrastructure." **Figure 2** illustrates the infrastructure at a typical repeater station.

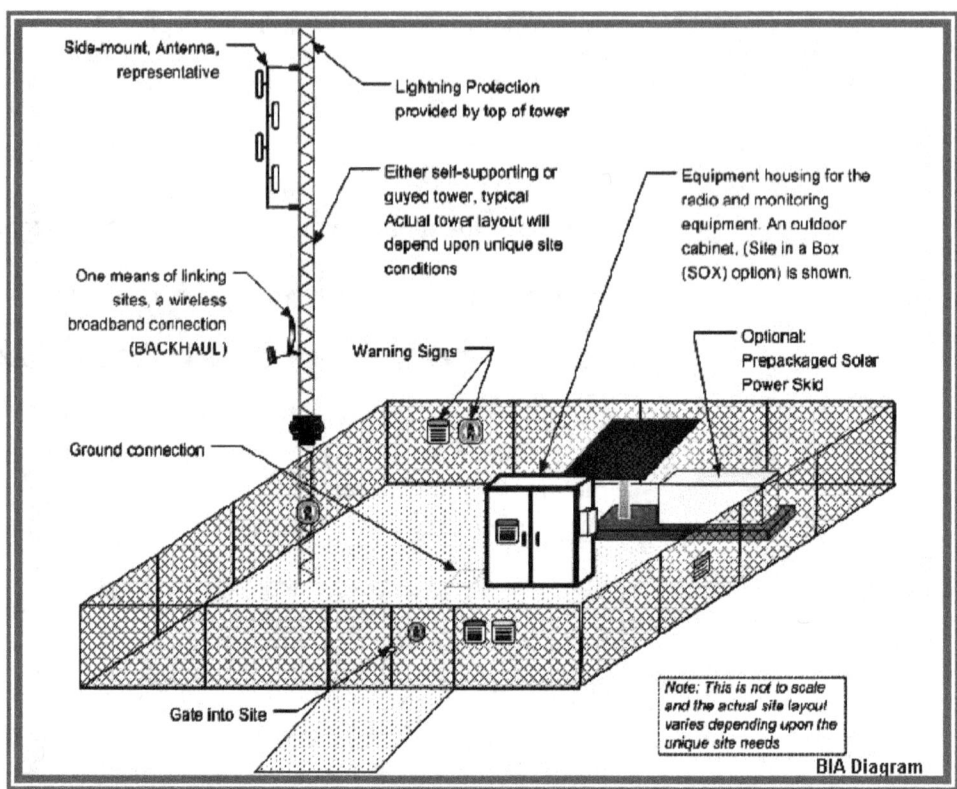

Figure 2 – Diagram of a Typical Repeater Station Detailing Required Infrastructure

There are a variety of radio technologies available, including analog and digital. Analog technology uses radio waves to transmit voice communications. Digital technology transfers voice communication in bits of information that are reassembled at the receiving end. While digital radios offer additional capabilities such as encryption, they also require more extensive infrastructure to operate. For example, digital networks typically require more repeaters and additional power to operate effectively.

Radios transmit signals on frequencies within specific bandwidths of the radio spectrum. Prior to 1993, very high frequency (VHF) federal radio systems used frequencies that were 25 kilohertz-wide (kHz). Since there are a limited number of 25 kHz frequencies within the federal radio spectrum,

2

the only way to increase the number of available frequencies is to use radios that can broadcast using reduced bandwidth. Reducing frequency spacing to 12.5 kHz (narrowband) effectively doubles the number of frequencies available within the federal spectrum.

THE NTIA MANDATED THAT ALL FEDERAL VHF RADIOS HAVE NARROWBAND CAPABLITY BY JANUARY 1, 2005.

The National Telecommunications and Information Administration (NTIA) manages the federal radio spectrum. In an effort to make more efficient use of radio spectrum, in October 1993, NTIA mandated that all federal VHF radios operate using narrowband technology by January 1, 2005. Both analog and digital radios can operate in narrowband mode. NTIA allowed agencies to decide whether to adopt analog, digital, or a combination of the two technologies to meet this mandate.

In 1996, the Office of the Chief Information Officer (OCIO) adopted the Association of Public Safety Communications Officials (APCO) Project 25 (P25) standards for digital narrowband radio equipment as the Departmental standard. P25 standards were developed to help address the NTIA narrowband mandate as well as to address the need of the public safety community for secure communications and the quality of digital transmission. One benefit of P25 compliant radios is that they can work in either analog or digital mode. In 1998, because of the perceived benefits at the time, the OCIO directed bureaus to transition all analog wideband LMR systems to P25 digital narrowband operation by January 1, 2005.

RESULTS OF AUDIT

DOI AND ITS BUREAUS
ARE NOT EFFECTIVELY
COORDINATING THEIR
TECHNICAL RADIO
SERVICES WITH
FACILITIES
MANAGEMENT TO
OPERATE AN EFFECTIVE
RADIO
COMMUNICATIONS
PROGRAM.

We found that DOI and its bureaus do not have an effective radio communications program. Specifically, they:

➤ are not updating aging and unsafe radio infrastructure,

➤ are not using their resources efficiently, and

➤ have not met the mandate to transition to narrowband technology.

The results of this audit demonstrate that radio communications in DOI are unsafe and unreliable because of three factors. First, poorly maintained infrastructure poses physical safety hazards and does not support reliable communications. Second, new radio technology adopted by DOI does not meet all users' needs. Third, DOI has a fragmented radio communications program that fails to connect the two critical components – infrastructure and equipment.

In addition to the safety and reliability issues, we also found that the OCIO's mandate to purchase advanced P25 digital radios resulted in the purchase of radios that did not meet user needs. Our audit identified the unnecessary expenditure of approximately $25 million at two DOI bureaus because of this mandate. Prospectively, we estimate that one bureau could still save approximately $10.5 million if it were exempted from this mandate in the future.

Finally, we found that DOI downgraded its radio communications program material weakness from a Departmental level to a bureau-level material weakness for only two bureaus, without conducting the required Management Review.

UNSAFE AND DETERIORATING INFRASTRUCTURE

DOI and its bureaus have allowed their radio communications infrastructure to lapse into poor and hazardous condition. The bureaus are not performing formal, routine site assessments to ensure the radio infrastructure meets Occupational Safety and Health Act (OSHA) requirements and they are not

4

taking action to mitigate known hazards. By its failure to mitigate safety hazards, DOI risks serious injury or death to employees and the public.

The Bureau of Indian Affairs (BIA) and the Bureau of Land Management (BLM) have begun to formally assess the current conditions of their radio infrastructure. During 2003, BIA hired an engineering firm to assess the safety and condition of its radio sites nationwide. The BLM Colorado State Office hired the same engineering firm to assess the safety and condition of all sites in its state.

The results were categorized as follows:

A   Excellent conditions with no safety or operational issues identified
B   Good conditions with only minor operational issues identified
C   Marginal conditions with several minor safety or operational issues
     identified
D   Poor conditions with several major safety issues and risk of injury or death
F   Extremely poor/hazardous conditions with immediate risk of injury or death

At BIA, 86 percent of its 157 radio sites nationwide were in poor (D) or extremely poor condition (F) with risk of injury or death. Only three percent were rated as excellent (A).

EIGHTY-SIX PERCENT OF BIA'S 157 RADIO SITES NATIONWIDE WERE IN POOR OR EXTREMELY POOR CONDITION WITH RISK OF INJURY OR DEATH.

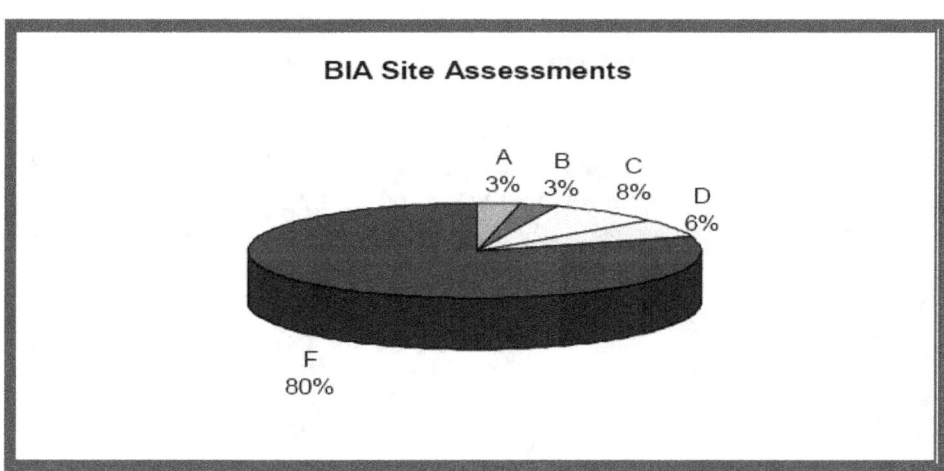

5

At BLM, 56 percent of its 16 radio sites in Colorado were in poor (D) or extremely poor condition (F) with risk of injury or death. None of the sites were rated as excellent (A).

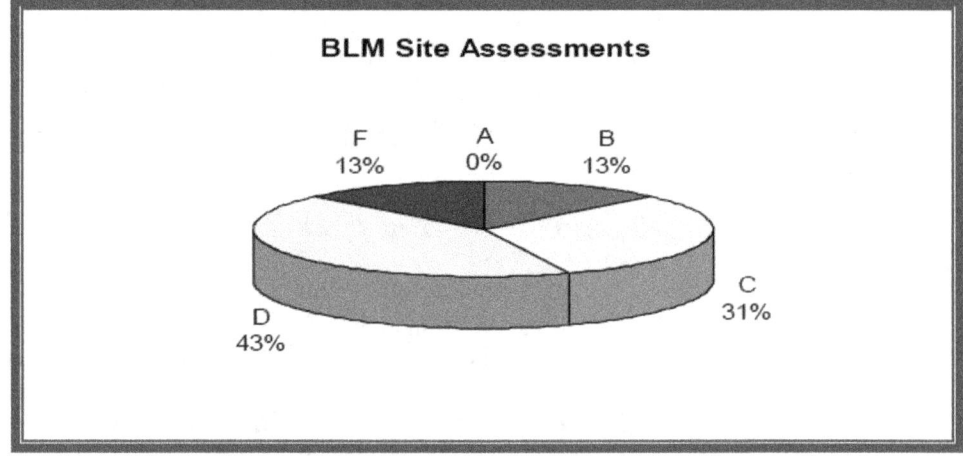

BLM Site Assessments

F 13%   A 0%   B 13%

C 31%

D 43%

During 2003, the BLM National Interagency Fire Center (NIFC) Wireless Group performed assessments at sites in **[Exemption 2]**. The group identified numerous safety hazards. For example, in Colorado the report stated: "It is apparent from the condition of some of the radio sites that proper maintenance, equipment upgrades and upkeep of these sites has not been performed for several years."

BLM also performed a comprehensive nationwide assessment of all towers supporting BLM equipment. As of December 2003, 58 (10 percent) of the 553 towers that support BLM equipment were considered to be in catastrophic or critical condition. In December 2006, DOI stated that only six towers currently remained in poor condition and that documentation on the current condition of these towers was available in BLM's Facility Asset Management System (FAMS). However, we found:

[EXEMPTION 2]

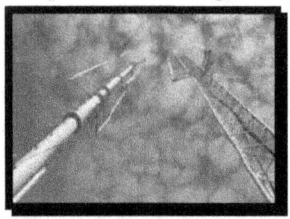

NEW TOWER (LEFT) ERECTED IN FY2004 NEXT TO THE OLD TOWER (RIGHT), BUT THE NEW TOWER IS NOT IN USE. THE OLD, UNSAFE TOWER IS THE ONE STILL BEING USED.

> FAMS data did not support that only six of these towers remained in poor condition. FAMS had inaccurate and incomplete information regarding tower condition. Less than half of the towers had records in FAMS. For those towers that were in FAMS, none were identified as being in poor condition.

> BLM radio technicians reported that at least 19 of these towers remained in poor condition, including 9 towers inaccurately recorded in FAMS as being in good condition.

This tower was built by stacking two components, making it unsafe to climb. Other than the attached notice, no measures were taken to restrict public access. FAMS lists the tower as in good condition, although it poses a safety hazard to both employees and the public.

This tower was not listed in the FAMS system, but has broken rungs and was in the 2003 BLM tower report as in critical or catastrophic condition.

THE FULL EXTENT OF THE SAFETY HAZARDS DEPARTMENT-WIDE IS UNKNOWN.

Since the number and extent of site assessments has been limited, the full extent of safety hazards Department-wide is unknown.

We reviewed BLM site condition reports and, with the assistance of bureau radio specialists, independently verified conditions at six BLM sites. We also visited one Bureau of Reclamation (BOR) site. Some of the safety hazards we observed during our site visits included:

- ➤ insufficient grounding of towers, antennas, and buildings;
- ➤ cables not properly installed and grounded;
- ➤ insufficient weatherproofing;
- ➤ improperly installed equipment;
- ➤ overloaded radio towers;
- ➤ no security fences; and
- ➤ equipment buildings in poor condition.

Overall, we found that the sites were unsafe for employees and the general public. The following examples illustrate the severity of the situation.

7

THE BLM CONTRACTOR
CONCLUDED THIS SITE
WAS IN SUCH A STATE
OF DISREPAIR THAT IT
"IS AN ACCIDENT
WAITING TO HAPPEN."

The **[Exemption 2]** radio site in **[Exemption 2]**, has an aged building with a leaky roof causing damage to the equipment. There are approximately 80 lead acid batteries being used at the site. Most of these batteries are poorly maintained, not protected, and corrosion is evident. Consequently, there is the potential of exposing employees and the public to harmful vapors.

Contractor Photos

The BIA contractor identified radio sites that had massive rodent infestations, including nests in the radio equipment and droppings throughout the buildings. The infestations pose a threat of rodents destroying electrical equipment and transmitting disease to humans.

Contractor Photos

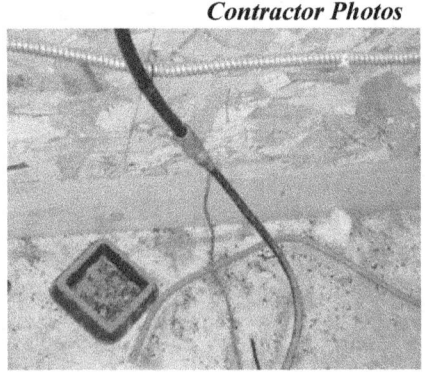

LIABILITY RISKS

Although most of these sites are located in remote areas, they are accessible to campers and hikers. There are roads and trails that lead directly to these sites. During our site visits, we observed evidence of the public using the land immediately surrounding the radio sites.

8

Failure to mitigate these known safety hazards makes DOI vulnerable to unnecessary liability arising from injuries to employees and the public. OSHA mandates the head of each agency ensure that employees have a safe work environment, develop a plan to address known deficiencies, and require that qualified personnel perform routine site assessments. Public access to these towers and facilities further increases DOI's overall risk of liability. Despite the contractor reports and the obvious risks to employees and the public, the bureaus continue to have difficulty obtaining the necessary funding to correct these infrastructure deficiencies.

To address these issues, management needs to develop a plan with dedicated funding to ensure the assessments are completed timely and corrective action promptly follows. Until corrective actions are completed, warning signs should be posted to alert employees and the public of identified hazardous conditions.

UNRELIABLE RADIO COMMUNICATIONS

We also found that DOI does not have a reliable radio communications system to support the safety of its employees and the public. This has become evident in emergency situations where individuals had difficulty communicating. There are three factors that negatively affect the reliability of the communications program.

> ➤ The infrastructure does not always support reliable communications.

> ➤ New radio technology adopted by DOI does not meet all users' needs.

> ➤ DOI's fragmented management of the radio communications program fails to connect the two critical components – infrastructure and equipment.

IMPACT OF INFRASTRUCTURE ON COMMUNICATIONS

In addition to the physical safety hazards already described, the condition of the radio infrastructure also affected employees' ability to communicate. If a repeater is not properly installed or maintained, this vital element of the network can render the user unable to communicate as intended. The following examples illustrate the significance of infrastructure as part of communications.

9

> In 2004, a BIA law enforcement officer at a remote site in **[Exemption 2]** was injured when attacked by a dog. When he attempted to call for help on his radio, he was unable to communicate because the equipment located at the transmission tower was improperly installed. As a last resort, the officer shot and killed the dog to protect his life. A passerby found the officer and was able to provide assistance.

> In 2003, a fireman in **[Exemption 2]** was on his way to an ongoing fire when he attempted to communicate information to dispatch, but was unable to do so from multiple locations. After over 3 hours of failed communication, the fireman ultimately had to find another crew to report to dispatch. Later he found out that he was unable to communicate because at least one of the repeaters in the area had been inoperable for some time.

MANDATED TECHNOLOGY DOES NOT ALWAYS MEET USERS' NEEDS

Published reports, and our site visits, also identified other communications reliability issues relating to the mandated use of P25 equipment. Users stated that the radios:

> were too heavy for people working in remote areas;

> were too difficult to operate for some users; and

> had insufficient battery life for use needed in the field.

The wildland fire community has an incident reporting system called SAFENET. In the SAFENET FY2005 summary report, communications incidents accounted for 38 percent of all reports filed that year. "Communications incidents" is one of six incident reporting categories -- which includes equipment failures or ineffectiveness as well as problems with personal communications between individuals. An increasing number of submissions highlighted difficulties associated with the P25 radio technology mandated by the OCIO. Many SAFENET reports demonstrate that P25 equipment led to difficulties in communicating during emergency situations and jeopardized employee safety. For example, in July 2005, a BLM helicopter manager reported that during the initial attack of a fire in **[Exemption 2]**, the handheld radio speaker stopped working. This resulted in having no communications with the helicopter, air attack, and other ground resources until additional trucks arrived on the scene.

10

The incidents reported in the SAFENET system are individually entered by staff as problems arise. However, the entries are not mandatory and individuals enter incidents as they themselves deem necessary, thus not all of the incidents may contain complete details. In fact, when we spoke with a fire safety management team in September 2005, they indicated that frustration with addressing communications issues in the SAFENET system has resulted in them hesitating to report problems at all anymore.

Another review performed by the NIFC Safety Team in September 2005, found similar issues such as:

- faulty equipment,
- battery limitations,
- radio incompatibility, and
- difficulty programming the radios.

During our site visit to the **[Exemption 2]** of the National Park Service (NPS), employees informed us that the limited battery life of P25 radios restricted their ability to communicate in search and rescue operations. Additionally, the radios did not provide adequate coverage to support researchers, rangers, and volunteers that work days at a time in remote and rugged areas. P25 radios require three to five times more batteries than analog radios for the same useful life. Some NPS staff require 80 hours of radio usage to be able to perform their routine field operations. The digital radios and batteries required for 80 hours of use weigh three to four times the weight of analog radios and batteries. The following photograph illustrates the difference in volume and weight that staff would have to carry in the **[Exemption 2]** for analog compared to two models of digital radios

11

P25 RADIOS REQUIRE THREE TO FIVE TIMES MORE BATTERIES THAN ANALOG RADIOS.

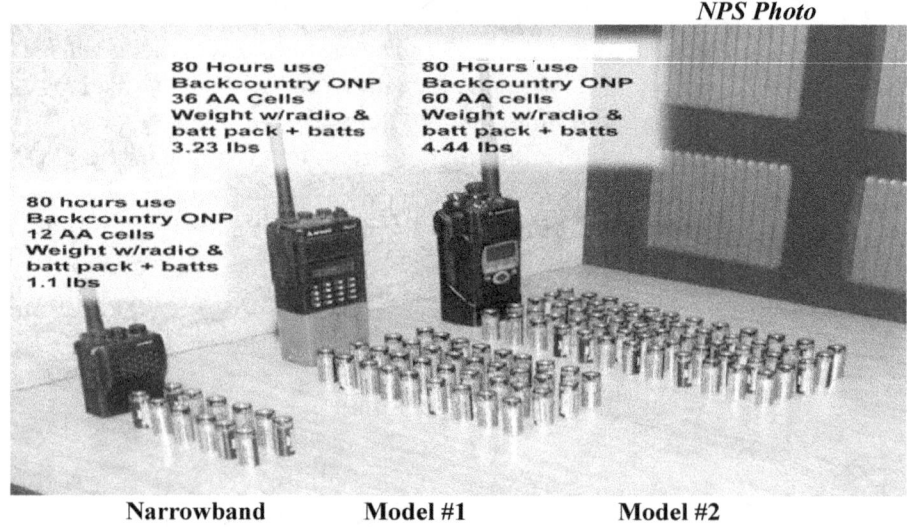

80 Hours use
Backcountry ONP
36 AA Cells
Weight w/radio &
batt pack + batts
3.23 lbs

80 Hours use
Backcountry ONP
60 AA cells
Weight w/radio &
batt pack + batts
4.44 lbs

80 hours use
Backcountry ONP
12 AA cells
Weight w/radio &
batt pack + batts
1.1 lbs

Narrowband	Model #1	Model #2
Analog	P25/Digital	P25 Digital

An NPS ranger told us that it is impractical to carry enough batteries to sustain sufficient communications in performing routine work such as day or overnight hikes into back areas of national parks. Instead, NPS employees limit the amount of time they use their radios, reserving them only as a link for help in an emergency.

In November 2002, NPS received a waiver from the Assistant Secretary for Policy, Management and Budget to purchase analog narrowband equipment for non-emergency service functions, such as maintenance and interpretation, rather than the mandated digital equipment. The justification for this waiver included ensuring that park non-priority functions continue and to prevent a communications breakdown. However, the OCIO informed us that it convinced the Assistant Secretary that allowing the bureaus to purchase the analog narrowband equipment for any reason would ultimately be a waste of funds. Although the OCIO could not provide any support that the waiver had been formally rescinded, the bureaus have only been allowed to purchase P25 radios. As a last resort, some NPS staff have purchased analog narrowband radios with their own money to ensure their personal safety.

USERS HAVE NOT ALWAYS RECEIVED ADEQUATE TRAINING

We also found that DOI and its bureaus often failed to provide adequate training when they purchased digital radios. According to the NIFC 2005 Fire and Aviation Safety Team (FAST) review, the P25 digital radios are difficult to program and DOI employees did not receive adequate training.

12

The group of field users told us that they have consistent equipment and field training for everything but the radio equipment. The Department allows the bureaus to purchase their P25 radios from a variety of approved manufacturers, which all have their own functions and style. The users are then expected to learn the radios themselves or get training on their own.

Technologically advanced radios provide little benefit if the infrastructure is not capable of supporting the advanced equipment and the users are unable to operate the radios effectively.

To remedy this situation, the OCIO needs to develop and implement a comprehensive radio communications management plan which would include, at a minimum, the following:

> addressing the deteriorating infrastructure,

> identifying the specific user groups,

> assessing the specific user groups' needs,

> ensuring all user groups are provided radios appropriate for their needs;

> ensuring all user groups are provided adequate training on radio use, and

> issuing and enforcing guidance that meets all of their needs.

WASTE OF DEPARTMENTAL RESOURCES

The OCIO failed to conduct enough due diligence when mandating that only P25 digital radios be purchased. This is evidenced by the fact that they implemented this mandate before the technology was fully developed to meet the P25 standard, the attendant infrastructure was upgraded, user needs were determined, and a cost-benefit analysis was performed. As a result of the OCIO's mandate, valuable resources were wasted.

Numerous problems were identified with the P25 technology, which resulted in additional expenditures. For example:

13

- Purchase of Replacement Radios: BLM spent an estimated $4.7 million on P25 radios recommended by the OCIO's working group that the users found inadequate because of battery failure, inadequate speaker volume, continuous feedback, and radio failure for unknown reasons. BLM then had to spend an additional $2.8 million for replacement P25 radios.

- Cost of Multiple Upgrades and Extensive Maintenance: At the **[Exemption 2]** and the **[Exemption 2]**, technicians have spent hundreds of hours upgrading the new P25 radios, costing almost $43,000 in labor. A bureau radio technician stated that "We're all short of time, money, and manpower and to have to spend [hundreds of] manhours simply upgrading radios . . . that is time away from important work."

  We found that over half of the P25 radio inventory at **[Exemption 2]** has not been able to be used for nearly 2 years because the radios are awaiting software revisions. The purchase price of this inventory is estimated at $456,000

NPS Photos

P25 Radios Valued at $456,000 in Storage Not Being Used

- Lack of Technical Expertise to Upgrade P25 Radios: NIFC reported that personnel at the BLM **[Exemption 2]** did not have the technical expertise, training, or personnel to properly upgrade their radios. As a result, in FY2005 they had to pay to ship 170 P25 radios to NIFC in **[Exemption 2]** for the upgrades.

- Purchasing Digital Capability Not Used: Digital radio communications require a more extensive network in order to receive an adequate signal over long distances and mountainous terrain. Mountainous terrain can, in some circumstances, restrict the digital signal. **Figure 3** illustrates how coverage gaps can occur due to

14

obstructions and the inability to place repeaters where needed. P25 digital systems are more prone to coverage gaps and thus require more repeaters than analog systems. In the absence of upgraded networks, some bureaus continue to operate their P25 equipment in analog mode. These bureaus are therefore paying for a more expensive digital capability that they are not using.

REPEATERS CANNOT ALWAYS BE PLACED WHERE NEEDED FOR DIGITAL TRANSMISSION DUE TO GEOGRAPHIC OR ENVIRONMENTAL LIMITATIONS.

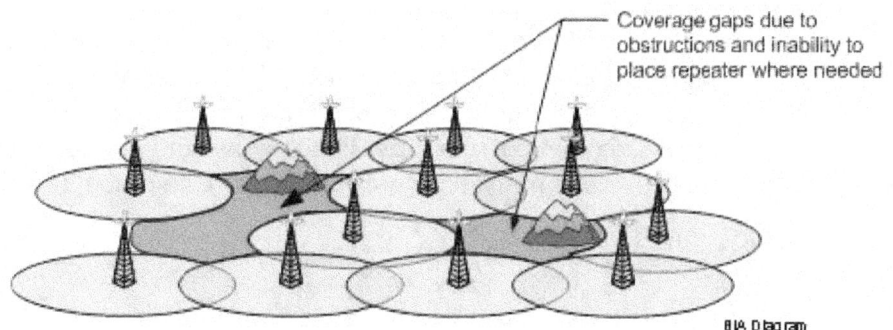

Figure 3 – Traditional LMR System Coverage for Network With Geographically Dispersed Users

The cost of P25 radio equipment is significantly higher – up to 24 times higher – than comparable analog equipment. A P25 radio costs between $1,350 and $2,897 while a narrowband analog radio costs between $119 and $770. P25 technology has not been sufficiently developed to justify the excessive cost for all users. By allowing the purchase of analog radios in appropriate situations, DOI could have saved between $580 and $2,778 per radio.

Below, we present two specific examples of the waste that occurred as a direct result of the decision to convert to P25 technology. In both examples, the bureaus could have purchased narrowband analog equipment to comply with the NTIA mandate, to meet users' needs, and to save funds. The additional $19.8 million spent on P25 digital radios by these two bureaus could have been spent more effectively to update their infrastructure.

THE P25 MANDATE RESULTED IN A WASTE OF $15.7 MILLION FOR BLM

"THE MANDATE WAS TO PURCHASE [P25 RADIOS], NOT TO USE THEM."
A BUREAU RADIO TECHNICIAN

BLM reported that as of September 2004 it had spent $22.9 million to purchase P25 equipment that it continues to use in analog mode. BLM's existing infrastructure is insufficient to operate effectively in the digital mode. Without an upgraded network, the encryption and other capabilities of P25 digital technology cannot be utilized. BLM does not have the necessary funding or plans to reengineer its existing infrastructure, let alone

15

acquire the additional infrastructure needed to operate P25 radios in the digital mode. BLM notified the OCIO of these issues, but the mandate to purchase only P25 equipment was never re-evaluated. The OCIO's rationale was that the P25 technology should work and they did not want the bureaus purchasing what they considered to be technology (analog narrowband technology) that was rumored to soon be obsolete.

BLM could have bought the same amount of analog narrowband equipment for $7.2 million, which would have saved $15.7 million since it began the transition to narrowband radios. These analog radios would have still complied with the NTIA narrowband mandate, and would operate with the same transmission capability as using the P25 radios in analog mode.

THE P25 MANDATE RESULTED IN A WASTE OF $4.1 MILLION FOR NPS [EXEMPTION 2]

As a result of the OCIO's mandate to convert to P25 radios, the [Exemption 2] of the NPS spent $8.1 million on radio equipment that did not meet user needs. The required P25 radios were too heavy, did not have sufficient battery life, and did not have adequate coverage to support the researchers, rangers, and volunteers that work in remote and rugged areas. [Exemption 2] could have purchased analog narrowband equipment that met its safety and practical needs and complied with the NTIA mandate for only $4 million.

These two examples identify almost $19.8 million of scarce DOI resources that could have been put to better use. We were unable to estimate the full cost effect of the P25 mandate because not all bureaus had comparable cost data available.

DOI COULD SAVE APPROXIMATELY $10.5 MILLION BY ALLOWING NPS TO PURCHASE ANALOG RADIOS IN THE FUTURE

NPS as a whole is only a fraction of the way through its transition to the mandated P25 technology, and many of its users throughout the country would have similar needs as the [Exemption 2]. We found that 60 percent of the NPS [Exemption 2] personnel were non-law enforcement and did not need the encryption or interoperability capabilities of the P25 radios. Using this as a baseline, we estimate that NPS in its entirety could save approximately $10.5 million (ranging between $8.2 million and $14 million) nationwide if it were prospectively allowed to purchase analog narrowband radios for non-law enforcement purposes.

16

FAILURE TO MEET THE NARROWBAND CONVERSION DEADLINE

DOI failed to meet the January 1, 2005 deadline to convert to narrowband radios. Only two of six bureaus, BLM and the U.S. Geological Survey (USGS), completed the transition and met the deadline. The remaining four bureaus are at various stages of completion. As of October 31, 2006, nearly 2 years after the required deadline, DOI reported the following implementation statuses for the four remaining bureaus:

> ➤ FWS 98% complete
> ➤ BOR 92% complete
> ➤ NPS 31% complete
> ➤ BIA 16% complete

Given all of the factors detailed in this report, we conclude that DOI missed the conversion deadline in part because the OCIO mandated P25 digital technology concurrently with the conversion to narrowband without adequately assessing the condition of the current DOI radio environment.

INAPPROPRIATE DOWNGRADING OF A DEPARTMENTAL MATERIAL WEAKNESS

In FY2000 through FY2003, DOI reported wireless telecommunications as a material weakness in its Annual Report on Performance and Accountability. DOI downgraded this material weakness in FY2004 from a Departmental level to a material weakness for only two bureaus – NPS and BIA. This decision was based on inaccurate information provided by the OCIO. The OCIO's Annual Statement of Assurance indicated that OCIO had conducted a Management Control Review (MCR) to justify downgrading the material weakness when in fact it had never conducted the review.

The results of our audit indicate that the radio telecommunications program should still be classified as a Departmental material weakness. Downgrading this weakness to only NPS and BIA was done without the requisite management review and thus, without basis to do so. Tragically, the downgrade may have reduced DOI's emphasis on improving this critical, but ailing, program. Therefore, DOI should re-instate radio telecommunications as a Departmental material weakness until the findings

17

in this report have all been addressed and corrected.

DEPARTMENT-WIDE APPROACH NEEDED TO MANAGE RADIO COMMUNICATION

STRUCTURE AND FUNDING OF THE RADIO COMMUNICATIONS PROGRAM
The radio communications program is classified as information technology (IT). Consequently, planning and funding for radio **equipment** is included in the IT Capital Planning and Investment Control (CPIC) process managed by the OCIO. Project approval and funding decisions for radio equipment are made by the IT Investment Review Board. However, the **infrastructure** is funded and maintained by the facilities staff. Any infrastructure repairs are approved by the Construction Investment Review Board process managed by the Office of Acquisition and Property Management (PAM). Facilities expenditures are managed through a 5-year Deferred Maintenance and Capital Improvement Plan that prioritizes facility projects for repairs, alterations, and new construction. **Figure 4** describes the separate processes for funding radio equipment and infrastructure.

HOW DID THE INFRASTRUCTURE GET IN SUCH A STATE OF DISREPAIR?

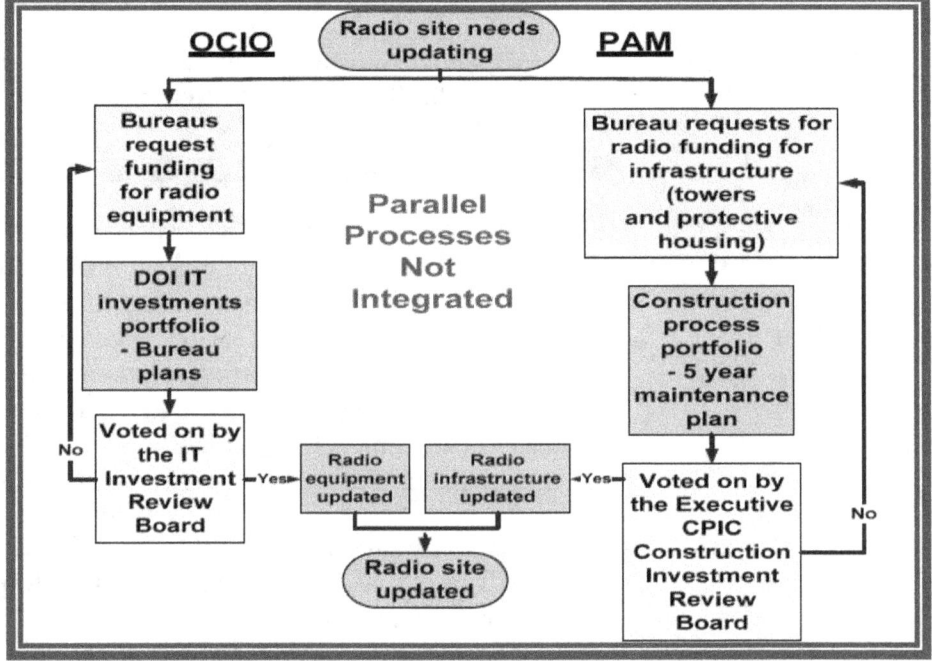

Figure 4 – Flowchart of Parallel Processes that are Not Integrated

An effective radio communication site must include the attendant

18

infrastructure and should be funded and managed as one unit. Since implementation of the Clinger Cohen Act of 1996, radio equipment and infrastructure have been managed by separate DOI entities – the OCIO and PAM. We found that the disconnect between these two managing entities is a major barrier in implementing a successful radio communications program. As a result of this approach, DOI's radio infrastructure is in disrepair, and the bureaus have been mandated to buy advanced technology that the infrastructure cannot support.

The OCIO informed us that it structured the radio operations in this manner to comply with Office of Management and Budget (OMB) requirements for separate financial reporting of IT and facilities investments. However, OMB informed us that the reporting mechanisms should not dictate who operates and maintains the programs.

We identified two federal agencies where radio communications were also vital to their program operations. The Department of Justice (DOJ) maintains and funds radio equipment and necessary supporting infrastructure as one overall program. DOJ believes that consolidated funding for radio resources and required infrastructure improves its program operations. Additionally, we found that the Department of Agriculture's Forest Service (Forest Service) includes towers as part of its radio equipment. The Forest Service has also found that having joint control over these critical aspects of program operations has helped maintain an effective, integrated radio communications system.

THE DEPARTMENT SHOULD BETTER UTILIZE ITS CPIC PROCESS TO MANAGE THE RADIO COMMUNICATIONS PROGRAM

The Department does not have a comprehensive plan for implementing its radio communications program. The OCIO focused its efforts on developing OMB Exhibit 300 as its overall planning document. However, OMB Exhibit 300 is only designed to coordinate OMB's collection of agency information for its reports to the Congress to ensure that the business case for investments are made and tied to agency planning documents.

Ironically, the OCIO has an award-winning[1] CPIC process that includes all of the components necessary to implement and operate a successful radio communications program. Although equipment and facilities requests go through the investment review boards, a key component of the CPIC process, DOI has not utilized all steps in the complete process for implementing its radio communications program.

Because OMB Exhibit 300 in itself is not sufficient as a planning document, the Department needs to prepare a comprehensive master radio communications program plan. This plan should include a capital planning process, investment analysis, life-cycle replacement, and implementation plans.

The CPIC process, depicted in **Figure 5**, would have captured many of the

19

components we found lacking in DOI's radio communications program.

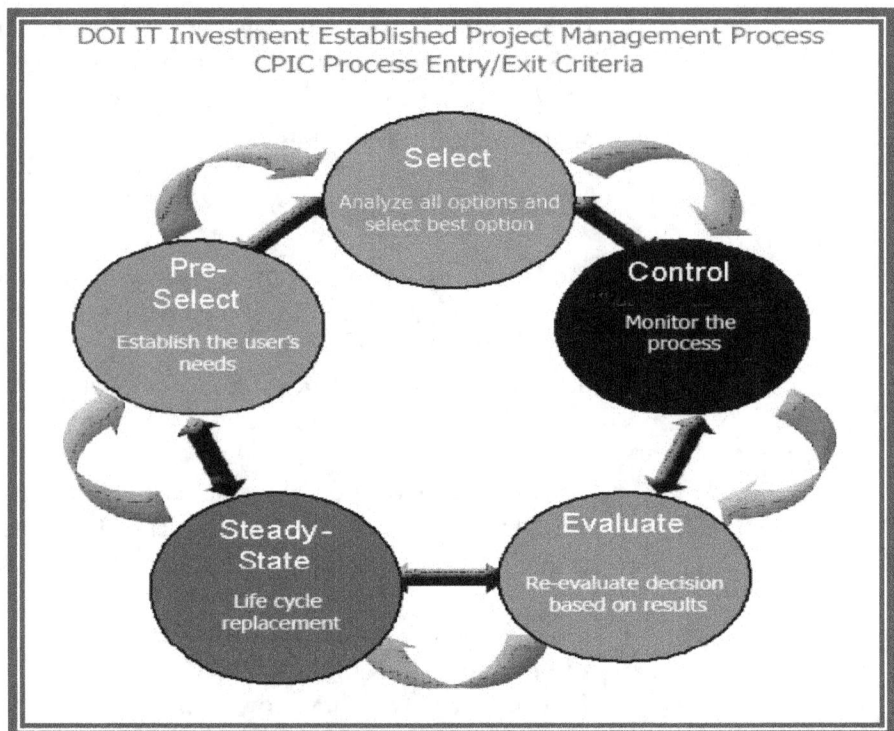

Figure 5 – DOI IT Investment Project Management Process

However, the OCIO did not address most of the steps described in the above process with regard to effectively managing its radio communications program, as follows.

> **Pre-selection – Establish Users' Needs:** The OCIO did not query the users to establish their needs. These needs varied among the different user groups. For example:

  - Law enforcement needs encryption capabilities.
  - Fire fighters need radios that operate in extreme conditions.
  - Back country users need long battery life and light weight radios.

> **Selection – Analyze All Options and Select Best Option:** The OCIO did not consider all options when mandating the emerging P25 technology—on its OMB Exhibit 300 business case analysis it did not consider narrowband analog technology because it had already decided to only consider digital technologies.

20

- ➢ **Control – Monitor the Process:** There was minimal evidence that the OCIO monitored how the new P25 mandate was affecting the bureaus' radio communications programs. The OCIO left monitoring up to the bureaus to implement and control the radio procurement and installation process with limited oversight and guidance.

- ➢ **Evaluate – Reevaluate Based on Results:** The OCIO has not re-evaluated its decision based on any feedback it received from the bureaus. The bureaus informed the OCIO of the infrastructure conditions and limitations and the continued problems with the immature P25 technology; yet the OCIO has not changed the mandate to purchase only P25 radio technology.

- ➢ **Steady-State – System Maintenance and Life-Cycle Replacement:** To date, DOI does not have a consistent radio equipment and system inventory to enable a life-cycle replacement methodology. On a bureau-by-bureau basis, there are ad-hoc stand-alone inventories but no centralized process or methodology to be able to effectively manage a reliable strategy.

The CPIC process also specifies that the IT Project Manager selected to manage the designated project be a trained project manager. The current radio communications program manager is not a trained or credentialed project manager.

STAKEHOLDER/USER SUGGESTIONS AND BEST PRACTICES

As part of our review, we identified suggestions from DOI employees, who are stakeholders and/or users of the radio communications program, and best practices used by other governmental organizations to improve program operations. The OCIO should consider these suggestions and best practices in developing its comprehensive plan to manage the radio communications program. A summary is listed below, and a detailed explanation is provided at Appendix 4.

MANAGE AS ONE PROGRAM	Departments that operate their radio communications operations as one overall program believe that having operations, maintenance, and funding for all aspects of the radio communications in one management function has improved operations.
ESTABLISH A CONSISTENT FUNDING MECHANISM	One long-range solution to improving and maintaining the radio system infrastructure would be to have dedicated maintenance funding managed by DOI's OCIO on a Department-wide basis.
ESTABLISH A LIFE-CYCLE REPLACEMENT SYSTEM	A life-cycle equipment replacement program that systematically tracks the condition and the useful life of the radio infrastructure would help project replacement costs.
CONSOLIDATE TECHNICAL SERVICES CAPABILITY	Centralizing radio technicians within a geographic area to track and maintain all the DOI radio systems within that area could reduce costs.
DIFFERENTIATE TRAINING BY USER GROUP	Each group of radio users has its own communication needs and level of experience. The various user groups should be identified and training should be developed as appropriate for each group.
SHARE INFRASTRUCTURE WITHIN DOI	DOI needs to encourage the sharing of existing and future infrastructure among bureaus to avoid duplication of effort and resources.
SHARE INFRASTRUCTURE WITH OTHER FEDERAL AGENCIES AND STATE AND LOCAL GOVERNMENTS	The bureaus need to take advantage of opportunities to share infrastructure with other federal agencies and state and local governments to reduce the overall cost of operating a radio system.
CONSIDER ALTERNATIVE TECHNOLOGIES	The use of alternate technology and initiatives, such as satellite systems, should also be considered when evaluating cost-effective alternatives to maintaining or replacing infrastructure.

RECOMMENDATIONS

We recommend the Deputy Secretary:

1. Reinstate wireless telecommunications as a Departmental material weakness until the findings in this report are sufficiently addressed and corrected.

DOI Response to Draft Recommendation: Did Not Concur

DOI stated that the Departmental material weakness should not be reinstated because DOI has made significant progress in its narrowband implementation. DOI also stated that it has made progress in addressing the condition of its radio facilities, including:

> ➤ BLM addressed the condition of radio towers cited in the report - only six towers remain in poor condition. Documentation on the condition of BLM towers is maintained in FAMS, which documents changes in facility condition based on work performed and updated assessments.

> ➤ Some bureaus indicated their radio facilities were in fair or good condition. For example, FWS completed comprehensive condition assessments for all of its facilities in 2006 and reported them in good condition.

> ➤ Bureaus are in the process of identifying inventory data on telecommunications infrastructure in the Federal Real Property Profile, including condition assessments for each asset. The bureaus have been specifically directed to provide complete and accurate information for this database.

> ➤ Bureaus have identified telecommunication infrastructure-related projects in their Deferred Maintenance and Capital Improvement Five-Year Plans and the establishment of policy requiring condition assessments be performed on assets with a current replacement value exceeding $5,000.

OIG Analysis of DOI Response: Recommendation Unchanged from Draft Report

DOI identified progress in narrowband conversion as the basis for downgrading the material weakness. However, the subject of the material weakness was the effectiveness of the radio telecommunications program, not the narrowband conversion. The narrowband conversion project was only part of the solution for improving the program.

23

DOI also stated that it made progress in addressing the condition of its radio facilities. It specifically cites progress made by BLM and FWS. We followed up on the condition of towers for these two bureaus and found that the assertions made in the response were inaccurate. Specifically:

> BLM: FAMS data did not support that only six towers remained in poor condition. Information provided by OCIO and BLM support that at least 19 of the towers remain in poor condition, including 9 towers that were inaccurately recorded in FAMS as being in good condition. We found FAMS data to be inaccurate, incomplete, and unreliable.

> FWS: FWS had not completed comprehensive assessments for all of its facilities in 2006. Only 49 percent of FWS' radio assets had current condition assessments. FWS stated that not all of the radio assets required condition assessments because of their low dollar value. Despite their low dollar value, the facilities that FWS has not assessed could have significant unknown safety hazards.

Even if DOI had addressed the physical safety concerns associated with its radio infrastructure, other significant issues remain that warrant reinstatement of wireless telecommunications as a Departmental material weakness. Specifically:

> DOI lacks a comprehensive radio plan.

> The new radio technology does not effectively meet users' needs.

> DOI continues to purchase P25 digital radios that its infrastructure does not support.

> DOI continues to have a fragmented radio communications program that fails to connect the two critical components – infrastructure and equipment.

> Four bureaus are not yet in compliance with the federal narrowbanding mandate.

2.   **Assign full responsibility over the radio communications program to the OCIO, including management and funding of all radio equipment and related infrastructure.**

DOI Response to Draft Recommendation: Did Not Concur

DOI acknowledged that some level of centralization of functions and funding was merited and that improvements were needed in the coordination of IT radio and facilities management. However, DOI stated that the recommendation was too broad and further study was needed to determine if aspects of the program should be centrally managed.

OIG Analysis of DOI Response: Recommendation Unchanged from Draft Report

In our opinion, coordination between equipment and facilities can best be achieved by assigning full responsibility for the radio program to the OCIO.

Once that has been accomplished, we recommend the CIO:

3. **Develop a comprehensive management plan for the radio communications program, with input from users and stakeholders, that includes the following components:**

   ➢ **The CPIC process to manage the radio communications program;**

   ➢ **A Department-wide action plan with milestones to perform necessary site assessments and correct deficiencies;**

   ➢ **A determination of the funding necessary to conduct site assessments, correct deficiencies, and perform routine maintenance on the radio infrastructure; and**

   ➢ **Short- and long-term strategies for completing the narrowband conversion.**

DOI Response to Draft Recommendation: Concurred

DOI stated that it is in the process of developing a strategic and operational plan.

OIG Analysis of DOI Response: Recommendation Unchanged from Draft Report

DOI needs to provide an action plan with milestones before we can consider the recommendation resolved.

4. **Identify specific user groups (for example, fire fighters, law enforcement, and biologists) and ensure the following:**

   ➢ **User needs are thoroughly assessed and addressed.**

   ➢ **Guidance that meets all users' needs is provided and enforced.**
   ➢ **All user groups are provided adequate training on radio use.**

25

> ➢ Allow users to purchase analog narrowband technology or to develop hybrid systems to address health and safety issues or limitations in infrastructure capabilities.

DOI Response to Draft Recommendation: Partially Concurred

DOI agreed that users should be included in developing policy, standards, procedures, and training. While DOI agreed there have been challenges in P25 implementation, it disagreed with removing the P25 standard to allow for the unlimited purchase of analog

narrowband technology. P25 is the de-facto standard for radio communications and has been adopted by 24 states and 14 federal agencies.

DOI stated that less expensive alternatives would result in only short-term savings that would not address interoperability needs. DOI stated that the draft report linked wasted resources to the P25 mandate without sufficient basis. DOI stated that the P25 standard should be retained with flexible implementation to address critical health and safety needs. Additionally, technological advances have lightened the available equipment and increased training efforts are addressing concerns related to P25 use.

OIG Analysis of DOI Response: Recommendation Revised Based on DOI Response

We revised the recommendation to allow users to purchase analog narrowband technology only to address health and safety issues or infrastructure limitations. We recognize that P25 has been implemented successfully in other organizations when adequately planned and funded. For example, the U.S. Forest Service had a 10-year implementation plan for fully transitioning to P25. If implemented, funded, and managed effectively, P25 compliant radios may be acceptable for most radio users. In the absence of an effective long-term plan, however, it is a waste of funds to force bureaus to purchase P25 compliant radios when they cannot be used effectively because of health and safety issues or infrastructure limitations.

5. **Appoint a credentialed project manager to oversee the radio communications program.**

DOI Response to Draft Recommendation: Partially Concurred

DOI stated that it would pursue the integration of credentialing programs for both program management and project management. DOI's response did not address the need to immediately appoint a credentialed project manager to oversee the program.

OIG Analysis of DOI Response: Recommendation Unchanged from Draft Report

26

The program has an immediate need for a credentialed project manager who already has the requisite skills to manage the program.

6.   **DOI should enforce existing safety procedures, such as posting warning signs, to inform employees and the general public of hazardous site conditions.**

DOI Response to Draft Recommendation: Did Not Concur

DOI did not concur with our draft recommendation to establish procedures to warn employees and the general public of hazardous site conditions. DOI and its bureaus have policies and procedures in place. It will engage the bureau Health and Safety Officers in ensuring any additional steps that are needed are taken to comply with these policies.
OIG Analysis of DOI Response: Recommendation Revised Based on DOI Response

We revised the recommendation to address enforcement of the existing safety policies.

7.   **Implement the following best practices, where appropriate:**

> **Establish a universal property management and radio system network database to better identify existing resources Department-wide and to help identify resource-sharing opportunities within DOI.**

> **Share infrastructure with other federal agencies and state and local governments.**

> **Consider alternate technologies.**

> **Centralize the bureaus' technical service capabilities to take advantage of expertise and resources Department-wide.**

> **Establish a consistent funding mechanism, such as a working capital fund, to ensure availability of funds for annual maintenance.**

> **Establish a life-cycle replacement program to systematically track the condition and useful life of the radio infrastructure so radio costs can be systematically projected.**

27

DOI Response to Draft Recommendation: Partially Concurred

DOI stated that it supports implementing best practices. It will expand its sharing of infrastructure, will centralize technical service capabilities and is developing a strategic and operational plan that will address funding mechanisms. DOI did not agree that it should implement a universal property management and radio network database.

OIG Analysis of DOI Response: Recommendation Unchanged from Draft Report

The radio program would benefit from the creation of a universal property management and radio network database. Information on radio equipment currently is kept separately by the bureaus using different systems, making it difficult for the OCIO to identify existing resources Department-wide.

OBJECTIVE, SCOPE, AND METHODOLOGY

The objective of our audit was to determine whether DOI and its bureaus are effectively managing the radio communications program. Specifically:

> ➤ Are they updating aging and unsafe radio infrastructure?

> ➤ Are they coordinating the use of existing resources?

> ➤ Has the mandate to transition to narrowband technology been met?

We examined the radio communications program operations for the specified areas above at the following entities: Office of the Chief Information Officer's (OCIO) Telecommunications Systems Division, National Park Service, Bureau of Land Management, Bureau of Reclamation, Bureau of Indian Affairs, Fish and Wildlife Service, the U.S. Geological Survey, and National Interagency Fire Center. We also relied on the work of a specialist in accordance with *Government Auditing Standards* issued by the Comptroller General of the United States.

To accomplish our objective, we:

> ➤ Reviewed laws, regulations, policies, and guidance relating to the radio communications program.

> ➤ Reviewed the business case documents submitted by the OCIO (OMB Exhibit 300) for the narrowband radio conversion effort for FY2000 through FY2004.

> ➤ Interviewed radio communications program staff and technicians and reviewed available budget and expenditure documentation as necessary to complete audit procedures.

> ➤ Projected the estimated cost savings of DOI implementing our recommendations by calculating the percent of non-law enforcement personnel at the remaining parks to be converted (60 percent). We then applied the ratio to the remaining parks to determine an estimate of non-law enforcement personnel needing radios. Finally, we subtracted the average cost of an analog radio ($433) from the average cost of a P25 radio ($2,017) to estimate the savings.

> Examined prior audit reports, Government Performance and Results Act goals, Departmental Performance and Accountability Reports, and various other reports issued by stakeholders providing suggested improvements on radio communications management.

> Reviewed existing bureau radio communications site assessment reports as available. These reports were prepared by either bureau radio specialists or by contracted specialists. We relied on these reports to draw conclusions on the condition of the sites assessed. We also verified the qualifications of the contracted specialists.

> Reviewed and considered radio communications management practices used by the Department of Justice and the Department of Agriculture's Forest Service.

> Performed tests of management controls sufficient to achieve our audit objectives.

We conducted our audit from February 2005 to December 2006. We completed our audit in accordance with *Government Auditing Standards*, issued by the Comptroller General of the United States.

We did not audit the radio universe or funding data obtained from the bureaus or DOI. We merely collected this data for background purposes.

We found issues specifically related to BIA that we will report on separately. However, we included BIA issues in this report that we deemed pertinent to the overall radio communications program.

DURING THE AUDIT, WE VISITED/CONTACTED THE FOLLOWING OFFICES OR ENTITIES [EXEMPTION 2]

[EXEMPTION 2]

[EXEMPTION 2]

ACRONYMS AND ABBREVIATIONS

AMCR	Alternative Management Control Review
APCO	Association of Public Safety Communication Officials
BIA	Bureau of Indian Affairs
BLM	Bureau of Land Management
BOR	Bureau of Reclamation
CIO	Chief Information Officer
CPIC	Capital Planning and Investment Control
DOI	Department of the Interior
DOJ	Department of Justice
FAMS	Facility Asset Management System
FAST	Fire and Aviation Safety Team
Forest Service	Department of Agriculture's Forest Service
FWS	Fish and Wildlife Service
FY	fiscal year
GAO	Government Accountability Office
IRM	Information Resource Management
IT	Information Technology
IWN	Integrated Wireless Network
kHz	kilohertz
LMR	land mobile radio
MCR	Management Control Review
MMS	Minerals Management Service
NIFC	National Interagency Fire Center
NPS	National Park Service
NTIA	National Telecommunications and Information Administration
OCIO	Office of the Chief Information Officer
OFMC	Office of Facilities Management and Construction
OIG	Office of Inspector General
OIRM	Office of Information Resource Management
OMB	Office of Management and Budget
[EXEMPTION 2]	
OSHA	Occupational Safety and Health Act
PAM	Office of Acquisition and Property Management
P25	Project 25
[EXEMPTION 2]	
RLO	Radio Liaison Officer
USGS	U.S. Geological Survey
VHF	very high frequency

PRIOR AUDITS

In the past 7 years, the Government Accountability Office (GAO) issued six reports related to DOI's radio communications program. In December 2004, the Office of Inspector General reported on DOI's use of wireless technologies. The following reports directly relate to the scope of our review.

➢ "Technology Assessment: Protecting Structures and Improving Communications During Wildland Fires," GAO Report No. GAO-05-380, April 2005.

Once a wildland fire starts, various parties can be mobilized to fight it, including federal, state, local, and tribal fire fighting agencies. The ability to communicate among all parties, known as interoperability, is essential. GAO found that this ability to communicate is hampered because different public safety agencies operate on different radio frequencies or use incompatible communications equipment. A variety of existing technologies can help link incompatible communications systems and others are being developed to provide enhanced interoperability. However, effective adoption of any technology requires planning and coordination among all agencies that work together. Without such planning and coordination, new investments in communications equipment or infrastructure may not improve the effectiveness of communications between agencies. DOI responded that the Wildland Fire Leadership Council has commissioned the development of a National Wildland Fire Enterprise Architecture team to improve interagency information technology and business practices. One of the focus areas for this effort will be geographic information systems used in wildland fire management by federal, state, tribal, and local agencies.

➢ "Telecommunications Management: More Effort Needed by Interior and the Forest Service to Achieve Savings," GAO Report No. GAO/AIMD-97-67, May 1997.

GAO stressed DOI's and the Forest Service's inability to aggressively share radio and telecommunications resources in an effort to reduce telecommunication costs throughout the two related Departments. GAO also concluded that DOI's Office of Information Resource Management (OIRM, the predecessor to the current OCIO), which had responsibility for managing and overseeing DOI's telecommunications activities has not exercised effective leadership by establishing a Department-wide program. Instead, OIRM relies on each of DOI's separate bureaus to identify and act on savings opportunities. DOI responded that it agreed to implement procedures within DOI and with Forest Service to ensure that all land mobile radio system designs are reviewed for sharing or other savings potential prior to radio purchase. DOI stated it is supportive of the goal of implementing shared radio systems wherever practical and cost-effective.

➢ OIG Report Number A-IN-MOA-0004-2004 – "Evaluation Report: Department of the Interior's Use of Wireless Technologies," December 2004.

We found that the Department's Wireless Telecommunications Program had a lack of: (1) planning for and managing wireless networks and (2) security provisions for wireless networks implemented by the bureaus. We found that DOI's management of wireless network technologies was not effective. Specifically, DOI had not acted in a timely manner to ensure that all wireless network devices were inventoried, wireless network technologies were researched and planned before implementation, and personnel were trained on wireless networks and security. DOI also lacked a systematic and comprehensive policy or approach to implementing wireless network technology. The OIG, among other actions, recommended that DOI establish a strategic plan to manage existing and emerging wireless technologies, including security provisions and methods for management controls. Although this report refers to wireless computer technologies, the OCIO Telecommunications Systems Division manages both this program and the radio communications program. This report identified a similar lack of comprehensive program planning and user training as we found in the current audit.

STAKEHOLDER/USER SUGGESTIONS AND BEST PRACTICES

As part of our review, we identified suggestions from DOI employees, who are stakeholders and/or users of the radio communications program, and best practices used by other governmental organizations to improve program operations. The OCIO should consider these suggestions and best practices in developing its comprehensive plan to manage the radio communications program.

MANAGE AS ONE PROGRAM

We identified two federal agencies, DOJ and the Forest Service, where radio communications are vital to their program operations and the safety of their employees and the public. We identified how they operate, maintain, and fund their radio programs. We found that DOJ provides all funds for radio equipment and required infrastructure to the radio communications program. This also includes managing any lease agreements for radio equipment on leased land. Having the operations, maintenance, and funding for all aspects of the radio communications program in one management function has streamlined operating this vital program.

The Forest Service includes towers as part of its radio equipment. The Forest Service has found that having joint control over these critical aspects of program operations has helped maintain an integrated radio communications system.

OMB stated that even though reporting requirements may be separate for IT and facilities, this does not mean that program management has to be separated as well.

ESTABLISH A CONSISTENT FUNDING MECHANISM

Officials in the OCIO recognized that the long-range solution to improving and maintaining the radio system infrastructure was to have dedicated maintenance funding managed by DOI's OCIO on a Department-wide basis. One option could be to establish a dedicated radio infrastructure working capital fund. This would ensure that funds are available annually for maintenance and not subject to discretionary use by the bureaus.

ESTABLISH A LIFE- CYCLE REPLACEMENT SYSTEM	Directly linked to dedicated maintenance funding is the need for a life-cycle replacement program. This program would systematically track the condition and the useful life of the radio infrastructure so that replacement costs can be systematically projected. As an example, the Forest Service used a life cycle program to track its infrastructure, repeaters, and radios with specifically identified replacement periods. The Forest Service believes this has enabled each of these programs to accurately assess, estimate, and track costs of current and future maintenance and upgrades.
CONSOLIDATE TECHNICAL SERVICES CAPABILITY	Currently, within the OCIO there is a preliminary proposal to consolidate all of the bureaus' technical service capability into one service center or task force. This concept would replace the current practice of each bureau having its own technical support staff. In this model, radio technicians within a geographic area would track and maintain all the DOI radio systems within that same geographic area regardless of which bureau uses the radio system.
DIFFERENTIATE TRAINING BY USER GROUP	Each group of radio users has its own communication needs and level of experience. The various user groups should be identified and training should be developed as appropriate for each group. For example, encryption capabilities and features that are important to law enforcement officers do not need to be included in the training for maintenance workers and summer park volunteers. DOI should also ensure that instruction manuals are tailored to the particular user groups and are easily understood.
SHARE INFRASTRUCTURE WITHIN DOI	DOI needs to encourage the sharing of existing and future infrastructure among bureaus to avoid duplication of effort and resources. In recognition of this need, the OCIO, with the cooperation of the bureaus' radio liaisons, started to develop a user-friendly database of infrastructure to better identify sharing opportunities for DOI. However, the project has stalled due to a lack of dedicated staffing to complete the project. Using DOI's existing property management system, Maximo, was also suggested as an option for tracking available radio inventory and equipment. Bureau staff agree that having a database is critical to their complying with the OCIO directive requiring all bureaus to identify opportunities for radio resource sharing.
SHARE INFRASTRUCTURE WITH OTHER FEDERAL AGENCIES AND STATE AND LOCAL GOVERNMENTS	Although analog and P25 technology each have their own strengths and weaknesses, both systems are still dependent on a network of infrastructure for effective radio coverage. Accordingly, taking advantage of opportunities to share infrastructure with other federal agencies and state and local governments is an effective way of reducing the overall cost of operating a radio system. The following examples demonstrate this practice.

> BIA and the State of **[Exemption 2]** have partnered to allow BIA to use the State's radio infrastructure. BIA plans to eliminate its unsafe radio sites in **[Exemption 2]** and use the State's system instead.

> A Federal law enforcement/emergency responder initiative, led by the Department of Homeland Security and DOJ, is the Integrated Wireless Network (IWN). IWN is intended to provide a consolidated infrastructure that will support encrypted P25 communications and provide a consistent framework for all law enforcement and emergency responder groups. This will facilitate reliable communications in emergency situations. This initiative has worked well in the Northwest, and may be applicable to all of DOI's law enforcement activities. The DOJ wireless program manager estimated that IWN had the potential to reduce its infrastructure network by half. To its credit, the OCIO has approved a demonstration project with this IWN initiative in the **[Exemption 2]**, which, if successful, may open opportunities for a Department-wide application.

All bureaus should be encouraged to look for sharing opportunities with other federal agencies and state and local governments. The OCIO needs to take advantage of these opportunities. GAO made a similar recommendation in its report titled: "Telecommunications Management: More Effort Needed by Interior and the Forest Service to Achieve Savings," GAO Report No. GAO/AIMD-97-67, May 1997.

CONSIDER ALTERNATIVE TECHNOLOGIES

The use of alternate technology and initiatives should also be considered when evaluating cost-effective alternatives to maintaining or replacing infrastructure. For example, the BIA Office of Law Enforcement Services in the State of **[Exemption 2]** determined that it was more cost-effective to equip its vehicles with satellite-linked P25 mobile radios when converting to narrowband rather than incur the cost of rehabilitating an aging network of repeaters. When officers have to leave their vehicles, they will have P25 handheld radios that can transmit to the mobile radio in the vehicle, which in turn sends the transmission via a satellite link to the dispatch center and other law enforcement vehicles.

38

SCHEDULE OF MONETARY IMPACT

Issue	Wasted Funds*	Funds To Be Put To Better Use**
Funds Used To Purchase Radios Not Meeting User Needs	$ 5,156,000	
Funds Used To Purchase Unused Digital Capability	19,800,000	
Allowing Remaining Parks To Purchase Analog Radios as Appropriate		$10,500,000
TOTAL	$24,956,000	$10,500,000

*   **Wasted funds are those funds which cannot be recovered.**

**   **Funds to be put to better use are those funds which could be saved if the recommendations are implemented.**

DOI's Response to Draft Report

THE DEPUTY SECRETARY OF THE INTERIOR
WASHINGTON

OCT 3 1 2006

Memorandum

To: Earl E. Devaney
            Inspector General

From: P. Lynn Scarlett
            Deputy Secretary

Subject: Response to Draft Audit Report, Department of the Interior, Radio
            Communications Program (Audit No. C-IN-MOA-0007-2005)

Thank you for the opportunity to comment on the Draft Audit Report on the
Department's Radio Communications Program. The Department agrees that
improvements can continue to be made in the areas highlighted in the report and
appreciates your comments and recommendations. In some cases, the Department has
made progress since the audit was initially undertaken. As a result, the conclusions
reached do not always reflect the recent progress made and current status.

The Department has made significant progress in narrowband conversion, which was the
basis for the downgraded material weakness. Only two bureaus have not completed
conversion. The Department does not concur that radio communications should be
elevated to a Departmental material weakness.

The Department is in the process of developing a strategic and operational plan that is
expected to lead to centralization of some IT radio functions. We agree that
improvements are needed in the coordination of IT Radio and Facilities Management,
including investment planning and technical assistance and guidance in reviewing the
condition of radio facilities.

In concert with the development of a strategic and operational plan for radios, the
Department will initiate an Internal Control Review to examine all components of the
radio program, including facilities. The Department will provide specific guidance for
the review, work with the bureaus to undertake a consistent approach across all bureaus,
and include a Departmental oversight team. Additional improvement activities will be
used to inform management and enrich our strategic and operational planning.

The Department disagrees with the recommendation to purchase analog instead of digital
radios for purposes unrelated to addressing health and safety issues. Short-term cost
savings in using analog radios would result in longer-term problems and impact
interoperability and effectiveness. While the Department agrees that some cost savings
and increased benefits could have resulted through increased coordination between radio
and facilities programs, as well as improved training and technical assistance, the

40

The Department is in the process of developing a strategic and operational plan that is expected to lead to centralization of some IT radio functions. We agree that improvements are needed in the coordination of IT Radio and Facilities Management, including investment planning and technical assistance and guidance in reviewing the condition of radio facilities.

We appreciate the review of our radio programs, the information contained in the draft report will assist us in successfully moving forward with improvements to our radio communications program throughout the Department.

Attachment

cc: R. Thomas Weimer, Assistant Secretary - Policy, Management and Budget
W. Hord Tipton, Chief Information Office

Comments on Findings

Clarify Affected Bureaus. The report should clarify which bureaus and offices are impacted by the report. The following bureaus and offices have radio programs: Office of the Secretary, Bureau of Indian Affairs, the Bureau of Land Management, the Bureau of Reclamation, the Fish and Wildlife Service, the U.S. Geological Survey and the National Park Service.

Facilities Findings Do Not Adequately Reflect Recent Progress. The report applies a blanket finding that all Departmental radio sites are failing due to maintenance neglect. The Report uses a 2003 BIA comprehensive baseline, a section of a 2003 BLM review and a single Reclamation site as basis for the finding. These evaluations cannot be used as a measure for the other bureaus' sites. In addition, BLM has made progress in addressing the condition of radio facilities and based upon your review does not warrant a conclusion that BLM sites are poorly maintained. BLM undertook a targeted effort to assess and improve the condition of its radio towers, and as result, BLM expects to complete improvements on the 57 towers noted in the draft report by the end of 2007 (six towers currently remain in poor condition). The draft report notes that no documentation could be provided that the towers were replaced or repaired, however documentation is available in the BLM's Facility Asset Management System, which documents changes in facility condition based work performed and updated assessments. In addition, project inspectors and Contracting Officer Representatives may have additional documentation supporting completion of work.

The Department and its bureaus have made significant progress on improving the management of its facility infrastructure. Over the past two years, the Department and the bureaus have implemented Asset Management Programs embracing the principles of the Federal Real Property Council established by Executive Order 13327 (Federal Real Property Asset Management). The Executive Order was signed on February 5, 2004. The Department's Asset Management Program is striving to achieve maximum use of real property, in terms of economy and efficiency, and to minimize expenditures for the purchase of real property.

The Department and its bureaus are implementing actions to ensure that assets critical to the mission, including telecommunications infrastructure, are sustained to fulfill the Department's mission. Progress in the past few years has been and continues to be made. Significant actions include the identification of telecommunication infrastructure-related projects in the bureaus' Deferred Maintenance and Capital Improvement Five-Year Plans and the establishment of policy requiring condition assessments be performed on assets with a current replacement value exceeding $5,000. The bureaus are in the process of performing these assessments.

42

In addition, inventory data on bureau assets including telecommunications infrastructure is updated in the Federal Real Property Profile. This repository of data on assets includes the condition index for each asset. The bureaus are currently updating this database and have been directed to provide complete and accurate data. Through the use of data in the FRPP and in the bureau-specific facility maintenance management systems, bureau managers are improving their capability to make good investment decisions on their telecommunications infrastructure and other assets.

Each of the Department's bureaus has processes in place to periodically assess the condition of their facilities, including radio facilities. The absence of special studies (like the BLM and BIA studies) of radio infrastructure in other bureaus is not sufficient to conclude that radio facilities are in poor condition Department-wide, particularly based on 2003 data.

In responding to your report, some bureaus also highlighted the need to revisit the finding on facility condition. They indicated that their radio facilities were in fair or good condition. For example, FWS radio infrastructure is reported to be in good condition. FWS completed comprehensive condition assessments for all of its facilities in 2006, and performs annual updates. FWS replaced the majority of its radio system infrastructure between 1999 and 2005.

P25 Standard. The P25 standard, is the de-facto interoperability standard via Public Law 104-113 that requires that *"all Federal agencies and departments shall use technical standards that are developed or adopted by voluntary consensus standards bodies, using such technical standards as a means to carry out policy objectives or activities determined by the agencies and departments."*[1] The P25 standard was developed due to failures in radio communications systems observed during incidents such as the Air Florida Flight 90 crash, the Oklahoma City bombing, the Attacks of September 11th, 2001 and illustrated more recently during Hurricane Katrina.

The P25 standard has been adopted in the following States: Alaska, Arizona, Colorado, Connecticut, Delaware, Florida, Georgia, Idaho, Illinois, Indiana, Kentucky, Michigan, Minnesota, Montana, New Hampshire, Ohio, Oregon, South Dakota, Texas, Utah, Virginia, West Virginia, Wisconsin and Wyoming. To assure interoperability effectiveness of communications to support national goals, the Department is working closely with these States, DHS, and others which requires adherence to the P25 standard.

In the Department's recently completed Radio Communications Partnering Analysis, "Top 20" States Radio Networks have been identified. The majority of these networks (16 / 20) are P25 based as well as digital P25 based (12 / 20) and should be considered as viable sharing opportunities with the DOI.

---

[1] PL104-113 12(d) – National Technology Transfer and Advancement Act

Federal agencies that have adopted the P-25 standard include the Department of Defense, Department of Energy, Department of the Treasury, Drug Enforcement Administration, Federal Bureau of Investigation, Federal Communications Commission (required for 700 MHz), National Institute of Justice, National Security Agency, National Telecommunications and Information Administration, Border Patrol, Customs, Defense Information Systems Agency, Immigration and Naturalization Service and the Secret Service.

The Department's narrowband strategy is a two pronged approach to achieve interoperability as well as spectral efficiency for radio operations. While the report is correct in pointing out that there are less expensive alternatives to meet the narrowband requirement these are short-term savings and the analysis does not address the need for interoperability. In weighing the benefits of purchasing P25 compliant radios, it is important to consider not only the costs of the radios themselves, but the benefits of interoperability and costs of non-interoperability, such as reliable communications in emergency situations. There are other costs that are more difficult to measure that result from maintaining multiple technologies including training, technical support, etc.

While we agree there have been some challenges in successful P25 implementation, the report should note that technological advances have lightened the available equipment. Increased training efforts in Interior are also addressing concerns related to P-25 use. DOI is planning another training event during the January 2007 timeframe. DOI agrees that training needs to be consistently implemented as well as recurrent to account for attrition and changes in the technology.

The draft report links wasted resources to the P25 technology mandate without sufficient basis. The cause of many of these findings may be more management driven versus technology based. On the "Purchase of Replacement Radios" section, it is not clear what the actual reasons for the radio failures were or whether the BLM sought the corrective actions that could have been provided through their acquisition office if in fact the radios received were defective in manufacture.

The report also refers to an issue relating to the "Cost of Multiple Upgrades and Extensive Maintenance" particularly for Yellowstone National Park and the Grand Junction Fire Center. It is stated that radios were kept in storage waiting on firmware upgrades and have not been used. While the new radios require more maintenance attention since they are now micro-processor based, upgrades are available, free of charge from three years of date of purchase.

In the Section on "Purchasing Digital capability Not Used," the first statement that "Digital radio communications require a more extensive network in order to receive an adequate signal over long distances and mountainous terrain" is

44

unsubstantiated. As illustrated below, P25 radios outperform analog radios in terms of decibel clarity and consistent power output.

Figure 1 - P25 / Analog Audio Quality vs. Attenuation (Daniels)

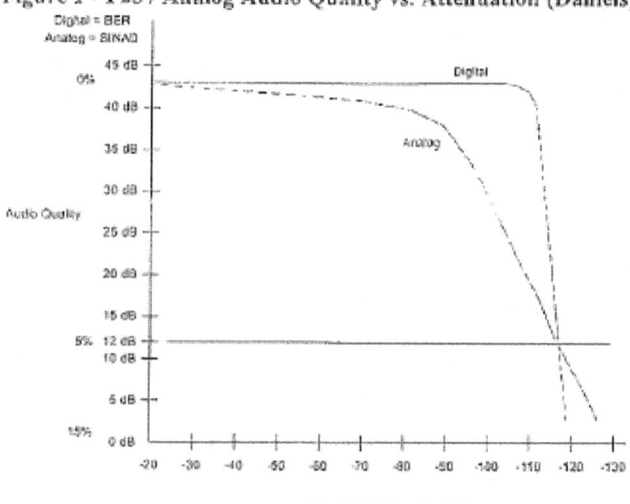

What the report may have meant is that P25 Radios are more sensitive to what is called "Multipath Reflections." Multipath reflections occur when the radio receives the same signal from multiple reflective sources such as mountains, buildings, etc. The use of a P25 system does not necessarily require additional sites, but as in any radio network, it requires that proper and thorough engineering be performed to achieve the greatest amount of coverage possible with the least number of radio towers. This is true in analog radio design as well.

The Department's strategic and operational planning process will address these issues.

Narrowband Conversion Status. The Department does not agree with the findings on the status of narrowband conversion.

The draft audit report includes outdated status as it pertains to the narrowband conversion deadline of January 1st, 2005. The Report states that the FWS and Reclamation were at a 70% and 55% completion, respectively.

While those percentage rates should be considered for that particular moment in time it should be noted that FWS and Reclamation are at 98%[2] and 92%[3]

---

[2] FWS response to Draft Audit Report, September 8, 2006
[3] BOR response to Draft Audit Report, September 8, 2006

45

completion, respectively and NPS has reported a 31.2%[4] completion rate. BIA is still at 16% however BIA will be completing conversion in South Dakota by November 2006. At that time, BIA's percentage rate will be increased to 26%. Additionally, it should be noted that Interior's timeliness in conversion is overall better than many Federal agencies. As of September, 2006 the following agencies have yet to completely convert to narrowband as well: DHS (40%), Justice (25%) and Treasury (23%).[5]

The completion of narrowband conversion will also be a focal area in our planning going forward.

Comments on Recommendations

Specific responses to the draft OIG audit recommendations are as follows:

➢ Reinstate wireless telecommunications as a Departmental Material Weakness until the findings in the report are sufficiently addressed and corrected.

Response: The Material Weakness was classified as a Department level weakness resulting from a management decision, based upon a 2000 determination that no bureau had completed its narrowband conversion mandate. The Material Weakness was reclassified in 2004 as a Bureau level weakness for the NPS and the BIA after all the remaining Bureaus were substantially complete in meeting the mandate. NPS and BIA were (and still are) considerably behind schedule.

These two bureaus will retain this as a material weakness. The Department will conduct Internal Control Reviews, and incorporate timeframes for completion of the conversion within the strategic and operational plan.

➢ Assign full responsibility over the radio communications program to the OCIO, including management and funding of all radio equipment and related infrastructure.

Response: While the Department agrees that some level of centralization of functions and funding is merited, the recommendation is too broad. The Department does not agree with the recommendation to move facilities functions and funding under the management of OCIO. Further study is needed to determine if aspects of the infrastructure program should be centrally managed. It is clear to us that a consolidated Exhibit 300 and a strategic and operational plan is needed that addresses communications and infrastructure.

The Department does support centralization of some radio functions under OCIO's recently established Technical Service Center, such as training, technical support, and equipment refurbishment. The Department will be pursuing appropriate centralization of functions consistent with its radio strategic and operational plan.

---

[4] NPS Monthly Status Report, August 29, 2006
[5] GMF Review – WPSMO C. Lewis 9/28/2006

The Department's strategic plan will guide the development of an operational plan that will build on the recommendations in a radio communications sharing partnering analysis that was completed in July 2006. This plan was developed, in part, based upon DOI Investment Review Board direction to complete an integrated facilities and IT plan for narrowband radios. Implementation of the plan is expected to improve the efficiency and effectiveness of the radio program Department-wide through an improved governance model and by taking advantage of sharing opportunities with Federal, State, tribal, and local cooperators.

> Develop a comprehensive management plan for the radio communications program, with input from users and stakeholders, that includes the following components: The CPIC Process to manage the radio communications program; A Department-wide action plan with milestone to perform necessary site assessments and correct deficiencies; A determination of the funding necessary to conduct site assessments, correct deficiencies, and perform routine maintenance on the radio infrastructure, and; Short- and Long-term strategies for completing the narrowband conversion.

Response: The Department agrees with this recommendation.

> Identify specific user groups (for example, fire fighter, law enforcement and biologists) and ensure the following: User needs are thoroughly assessed and addressed; Guidance that all users' needs is provided and enforced; All user groups are provided adequate training on the use of radios; and allow users to purchase analog narrowband technology or to develop hybrid systems if it is determined that analog technology better suits the needs of a particular user group;

Response: Agree that stakeholder involvement is needed. Users should be included in developing policy, standards, procedures, as well as training. We disagree with removing the P25 standard to allow for the unlimited purchase of analog narrowband technology. The P25 standard should be retained with flexible implementation to address critical health and safety needs.

> Appoint a credentialed project manager to oversee the program.

Response: We agree that additional integration of credentialing is required for program management as well as project management. DOI will be pursuing both levels of credentialing through the Project Management Institute. DOI is structuring the program to utilize in-house Project Management Professionals (PMPs) and contracted PMPs when required for development, modernization or enhancement (DME) related activities (such as narrowbanding and 1710 Spectrum Relocation).

> Establish procedures, such as posting warning signs, to inform employees and the general public of hazardous site conditions.

47

· **Response:** The Department and its bureaus have policies and procedures in place for this. The Department will engage the Bureau Health and Safety Officers in ensuring any additional steps that are needed are taken to comply with these policies.

➢ Implement the following best practices, where appropriate: Establish a universal property management and radio network database to better identify existing resources Department-wide and to help identify resource sharing opportunities within DOI; Share infrastructure with other federal agencies and state and local governments; Consider Alternate technologies; Centralize the Bureau's technical service capabilities to take advantage of expertise and resources Department-wide; Establish a consistent funding mechanism, such as a working capital fund, to ensure availability of funds for annual maintenance, and; Establish a life cycle replacement program to systematically track the condition and useful life of radio infrastructure so radio costs can be systematically projected.

Response: The Department does not agree that we should implement a universal property management and radio network database. The Department supports implementing best practices. The Department already extensively shares infrastructure and will expand sharing. We are planning to centralize technical service capabilities. We will determine the resources needed centrally or in the bureaus based upon a strategic and operational plan that will form the basis for the determining funding mechanisms.

STATUS OF AUDIT RECOMMENDATIONS

Recommendations	Status	Action Required
1 and 2	Unresolved Management did not concur	Reconsider the recommendations; provide a written response stating concurrence or non-concurrence; and provide information on actions taken or planned, including target dates and titles of the officials responsible for implementation.
3	Unresolved Management concurred; additional information needed	Provide information on actions taken or planned, including target dates and titles of the officials responsible for implementation.
4	Unresolved Management partially concurred; recommendation revised	Consider the revised recommendation; provide a written response stating concurrence or non-concurrence; and provide information on actions taken or planned, including target dates and titles of the officials responsible for implementation.
5 and 7	Unresolved Management partially concurred	Reconsider the recommendations; provide a written response stating concurrence or non-concurrence; and provide information on actions taken or planned, including target dates and titles of the officials responsible for implementation.

Report Fraud, Waste, Abuse, and Mismanagement

Fraud, waste, and abuse in government concerns everyone: Office of Inspector General staff, Departmental employees, and the general public. We actively solicit allegations of any inefficient and wasteful practices, fraud, and abuse related to Departmental or Insular Area programs and operations. You can report allegations to us in several ways.

By Mail: U.S. Department of the Interior
Office of Inspector General
Mail Stop 5341 MIB
1849 C Street, NW
Washington, D.C. 20240

By Phone   24-Hour Toll Free   800-424-5081
Washington Metro Area   703-487-5435

By Fax   703-487-5402

By Internet   www.doioig.gov/hotline

50

www.ingramcontent.com/pod-product-compliance
Lightning Source LLC
Chambersburg PA
CBHW080549290526
45790CB00006B/2602